D1104617

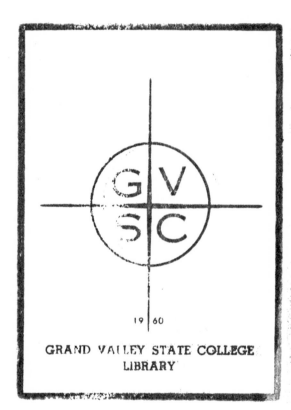

# What's
# Happening?

Material contributed by
Bob Orben and Jim Sanders

What's happening?

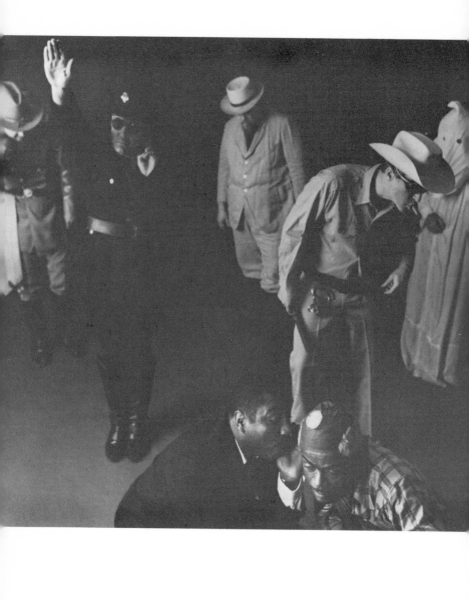

A house divided cannot stand

"We Shall Overcome"

# *What's Happening?*

## by DICK GREGORY

PHOTOGRAPHS BY JERRY YULSMAN

E. P. DUTTON & CO., INC.
New York  1965

Published simultaneously in Canada by Clarke, Irwin & Company Limited,
Toronto and Vancouver

*Library of Congress Catalog Card Number: 65-19973*

## *Dedication*

To Benny Dunn and Earl Wilson who, of all people so instrumental to my early career, were left out of my autobiography. I beg their pardon for omitting mention of their names, while listing those to whom I owe my gratitude, with an excuse proportionate to their kindness and encouragement: that I did so because it was beyond words and saved them to put into the pictures.

Also by Dick Gregory

FROM THE BACK OF THE BUS

*nigger*

# What's
# Happening?

*How to recognize an Uncle Tom*

Uncle Tom football player . . .

Uncle Tom cop . . .

Uncle Tom marine . . .

Uncle Tom preacher . . .

Had Napoleon been an Uncle Tom . . .

Had General Custer been an Uncle Tom . . .

"No more Uncle Tom-tom"

The answer to the racial problem is simple—it's give and take. If they don't give it, we're going to take it!

The hope is with the kids.

All your life, Reverend, you've been telling people "Thou shalt not kill," and you're going to lead me to the killer!

*Anything more I can do for you, son?*

Yes, Father, come in here and hold my hand.

*Our Alternate Sponsor—The Supreme Court*

In a way, it's kind of fitting. Men in white sheets took our rights away—and now, men in black sheets are giving them back.

And after tangling with Southern justice, it's a pleasure to know there's a court where you *feel* like standing when the judge comes in.

Any friend of Sammy Davis, Jr., is a friend of mine.

I hate to go to Miami in the wintertime because when I come back home I can't prove it. I mean the sun don't do nuthin for me. But I have a lot of fun going out to the beach every day, looking at the white folks laying in the sun trying to outblack one another.

I go to the same beach every night and lay in the moon.

I've always been one of those colored cats that never admitted I was colored if I didn't have to. When applying for a job, I used to *mail* the application in. In filling out the section in the application that said "color," I used to put "off-white"—and let them guess how far off it was.

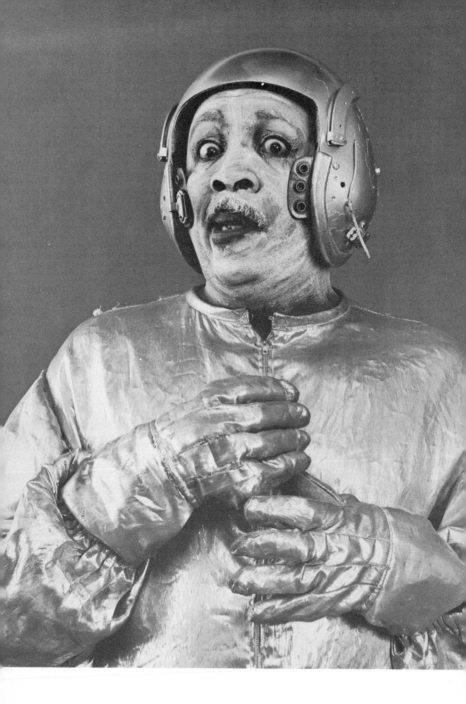

I'll do anything to be the first Negro astronaut, to show the world what true guts really looks like.

A lot of people think it takes a lot of guts for one of these astronauts to jump in the rocket and they blast him off, but to me true guts would be for one of those astronauts to chicken out five minutes before flight time—on national TV. "I ain't goin—damn that ticker-tape parade."

Can you imagine the first Negro astronaut going around the world? And the people of Perth turning on their lights so he knows where he is . . .

. . . and the people of South Africa turning them off—so he'll know where he'd better not be.

*My Favorite Sport*

Football is my favorite sport, the only sport in the world where a Negro can chase a white man and 40,000 people stand up and cheer.

If I didn't have my hat on, they'd be calling me Nappyoleon.

You know what I can't understand? If basic black has always been fashionable in clothes—why not in people?

Is it true blondes have more fun?

You gotta take some of what's happening with a little grain of salt. Like two of us met on the street this morning, and the first one said, "Man, wasn't it awful how that spontaneous, unplanned, unpremeditated riot started last night?" And the other one answered, "Shhhh. It's tonight!"

*The Long Hot Summer—Harlem, 1964*

The Negroes had the bottles, and the cops had the bazookas and Martin Luther King came in and said: "Cool it, baby, we're winning."

We found out later he was talking to the cops.

Hey, officer, would you bust these watermelons for me?

*I'm sorry, we thought you were a demonstrator. We didn't
know you were the neighborhood bookie.*

In the parks in New York the only ones holding hands after midnight are the cops!

Man, it's getting so bad, one night alone eight people yelled for the fuzz—and three of them were muggers!

And there was the time the cops got a phone call, and a frantic voice said, "You gotta get me out, I tell ya. You gotta get me out! I can't stand another night in this park!" The sergeant said, "Would you speak a little louder?" The voice said, "I can't. I'm a tree."

Business

*Credit: Fredrick Douglas De Van*

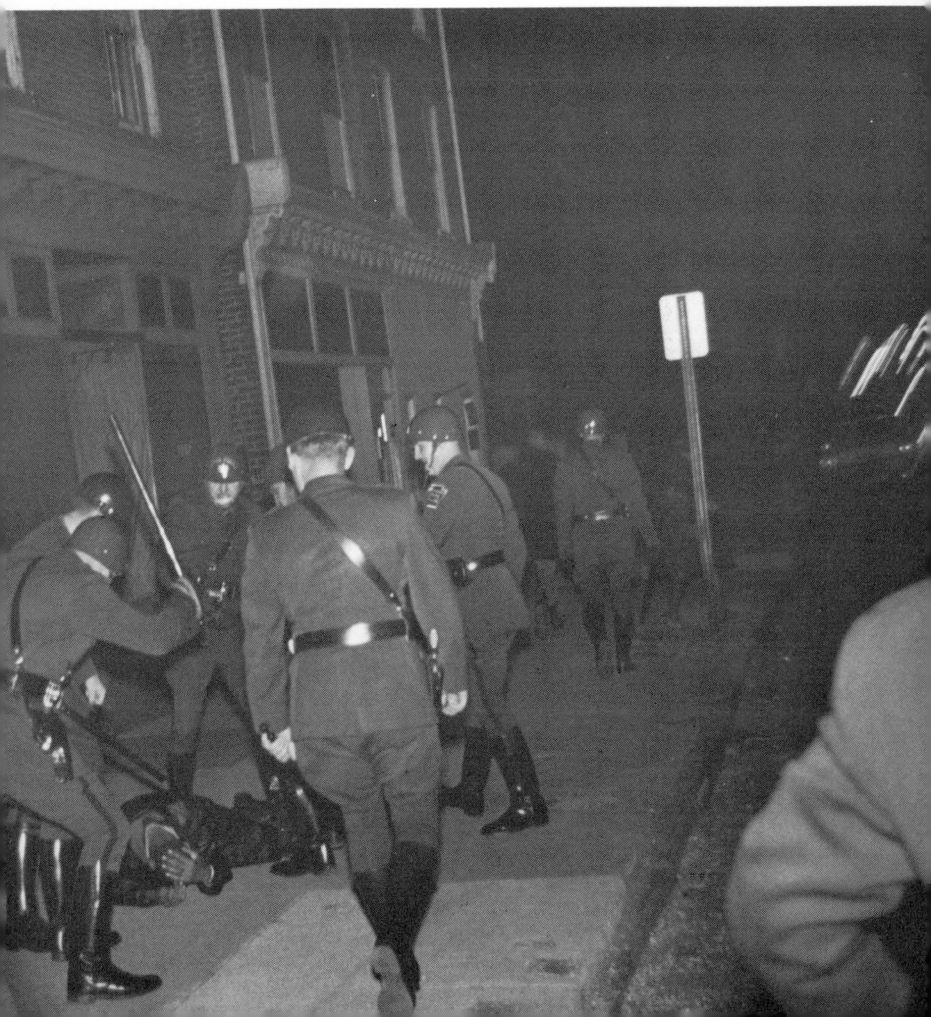

before pleasure

*Credit: Fredrick Douglas De Van*

What demonstrations, lady? You've got your Kings mixed up.

Sheriff, why do you want to waste tear gas on us? We got enough to cry about already.

*Going to the Courthouse to register, boy?*

No, sir, to pay my taxes.

If it wasn't for that sheriff and his club I wouldn't have had no medical deductions this year at all. Every time his club goes up, up, up, my taxes go down, down, down.

Did you hear about the two Southern crackers who had never heard of an eclipse? They're working in a field, and suddenly the sun starts to disappear. Terrified, they fall to their knees and start praying. "Oh, Lord," one of them is saying, "protect me from this evil and I will never smoke or chew again!" But the sun keeps getting darker. "Lord, save me, and I will never curse or blaspheme again!" Darker yet. "And I won't cheat, steal, lie or carry on with painted women!" Now the sun is completely blotted out and this fella is desperate. "Lord, hear me, Lord. Deliver me, and I will never lay a hand on another nigger so long as I live!"

And, suddenly, the sun starts coming out. The farmer is dumbfounded. He nudges the other cracker and says, "Zeke! Zeke, you figure this means Dick Gregory's right?"

*What'd you give up for Lent, boy?*

Nonviolence!

*Stand back, there, y'all. I told you you'll make that five-day march to Montgomery over my dead body.*

Baby, that wouldn't be a bad route.

*Selma*

And then we marched, and Governor Wallace was scared and nervous.

As a matter of fact, he was so scared he put Alabama in his wife's name.

*Credit: Laurence Henr*

The first day of the march, Governor Wallace said: "That rabble-rousing mob has just left Selma."

Credit: Laurence Hen

The second day of the march, Wallace said: "Those outside agitators have marched twenty miles."

Credit: Laurence He

The third day of the march, Wallace said: "Those civil-rights workers are halfway here."

Credit: Laurence H

The fourth day, he said: "Those Freedom Fighters are right outside Montgomery."

*Credit: Laurence Her*

On the fifth day . . .

Governor Wallace looked out the State House window and dug that crowd and said: "Hey, baby, what took y'all so long?"

*Credit: Laurence Henry*

Hey, old man, why are you marching five days to Montgomery?

*So my boys won't have to shuffle for another hundred years.*

Stop the world, I want to get on!

What's happening, baby?

*White man take my woman, white man kill buffalo, white man
break treaty!*

87

Cool it, baby. I'm with *you*.

*Have demonstrations hurt your career?*

I won't say demonstrations haven't affected my way of life a little. Some families have sleep-in maids. We have sleep-in bail bondsmen.

*Making a Movie*

I've just finished making a movie for Hollywood. The name of the movie is *White Like You*. This is the story of a Mississippi sharecropper who painted himself white and moved to Arizona . . .

. . . and got tomahawked to death by a nervous Indian—

and I played the part of the Indian.

Putting us in movies is really making them a lot more realistic. For instance, now you go to see a Western, and if there's a cat named Black Bart—he is!

And then he says, "Ah reckon I'll mosey down to the Last Chance Saloon."

"You going in for a drink?"

"In Texas? It's dangerous enough just to mosey!"

Do you realize Red China has 688,000,000 people? If those cats ever start singing "We Shall Overcome," they're gonna *do* it.

Things are so confused, we don't know whether to teach the troops to drink vodka, speak Spanish or eat rice.

Every time Red China blasts off a nuclear bomb, our State Department calls it primitive. I called Dean Rusk and asked him, "How you gonna call Red China's nuclear blast primitive and you scared of my switchblade?"

He informed me that he was not referring to Red China's nuclear blast as being primitive, but through our intelligence we had found out it would take Red China twenty to thirty years to develop the vehicle to deliver that bomb over here.

And I told him, with 688,000,000 people they can *hand-*carry that bomb over here.

Remember when Custer called Sitting Bull primitive?

Have you ever noticed the way big business takes everything in its stride? Like, there's a huge Chicago company that's going along with integration 100 percent. They're replacing half their white workers with colored machines.

And I understand a Southern company just came up with the world's first colored computer. It does everything the other computers do—but they only have to give it half the current.

We have always underestimated people. Remember when that scientist told George Washington Carver, "Get out of here, boy, and take your peanuts with you"?

*Jailbreak*

*I'll teach you about breaking outa jail. Where's the rest of them niggers?*

I always believe in upholding law and order.

*You're a good boy. They all ought to be like you.*

*You Communist!*

*You can't marry my sister, but if you're as rich as you look, you can marry* me.

We're doing all right. At the rate they're hiring us today, ten years from now there won't be enough of us to go around. It won't be nuthin to drive down the street and see a big sign reading: "Hertz Rent-a-Negro—for all occasions."

## Acknowledgments

My thanks to all those who helped with the pictures in this book, especially Earl Hammond who took the part of the Sheriff, and everyone on the Selma march:

EDWARD BELINSKI

BRYON COLEMAN

BERK COSTELLO

EARL DOWD

KENT DRAKE

MRS. BOBBI FELDMAN

EARL HAMMOND

REV. JAMES R. MCGRAW

W. R. MUNROE

ARTHUR STEUER

JERRY YULSMAN